Simple Solutions™

Socialization

By
Kim Campbell Thornton
Illustrations by Buck Jones

Plus Training Tips

BOWTIE
PRESS®

A Division of BowTie, Inc.
Irvine, California

Karla Austin, *Business Operations Manager*
Nick Clemente, *Special Consultant*
Kendra Strey, *Project Editor*
Honey Winters, *Design*
Cover and book design concept by Michael V. Capozzi

The dogs in this book are referred to as *he* and *she* in alternating chapters.

Library of Congress Cataloging-in-Publication Data

Thornton, Kim Campbell.
  Socialization / by Kim Campbell Thornton ; illustrations by Buck Jones.
    p. cm. — (Simple solutions)
  ISBN 1-931993-78-5
  1. Dogs—Training. 2. Dogs—Social aspects. I. Title. II. Series: Simple solutions (Irvine, Calif.)

  SF431.T5346 2006
  636.7088'7—dc22
                    2006002804

BowTie Press®
A Division of BowTie, Inc.
3 Burroughs
Irvine, California 92618

Printed and bound in Singapore
10 9 8 7 6 5 4 3 2 1

Contents

What Is Socialization?

Dogs are known as man's best friend, but they don't come ready-made to take on this role. If they're to become accustomed to life with people, dogs need to be exposed to people's touch, sight, and sounds; this begins with proper socialization at birth. Socialization is the process of training a dog to live in a social environment— one that includes people, other dogs, and other animals such as cats or horses. Dogs are naturally social animals. Wild dogs live in packs that are similar to human families:

they have a male leader (alpha male), a female leader (alpha female), and other pack members who fall under the alphas in the hierarchy. Alphas lead hunts, produce offspring, and decide where the pack lives.

Generally, domestic dogs no longer live in true packs, except during puppyhood when they learn the basics of being a dog from their interactions with their mother and their littermates. When puppies go to live with their new families, they must learn their place in the human "pack." Introducing puppies to human sound and touch during their various developmental stages helps the pups to

recognize people as leaders as well as to understand human body language and vocal tones. This is the key to teaching them what they need to know to have fulfilling home lives.

It's important for us to understand a dog's social needs and the stages of canine emotional development in order to properly socialize a dog. The time between the newborn stage and the adult stage is full of change. In the following chapter, we will take a look at these various developmental periods.

Puppy Life Stages

Dogs go through five stages of emotional development: newborn (neonatal), transition, socialization, adolescent (juvenile), and adult.

Pretty much all newborn puppies do is eat and sleep. For their first two weeks of life, puppies are blind and deaf. They don't move much, except to find their mother's milk-producing nipple.

In the transitional third week, the eyes open, the ears become functional, and baby teeth emerge. Puppies in

this transitional period are capable of learning. For example, they learn to associate certain behaviors with food rewards and pain with avoidance.

The socialization stage, which begins after the transitional third week and lasts through twelve weeks of age, is the time of greatest influence on puppies. Through play with their littermates, puppies develop physical coordination, learn pack hierarchy, and quickly come to find that biting too hard is a no-no. This is the time to introduce puppies to household and outdoor sounds and objects as well as to make introductions to new people, such as the veterinarian and potential puppy buyers. For these reasons, many breeders keep puppies with their littermates until they're at least twelve weeks old. Puppies still sleep a lot, but there's a change in their brain wave activity while they're awake. The brain waves become much greater in amplitude, likely a result of the new abilities of sight and hearing. During this stage, puppies learn to run, bark, wag their tails, and make different facial expressions using their ears and lips to communicate.

Even after the traditional "end" of the socialization period at twelve weeks, puppies continue to learn. Now

is not the time to slack off on socialization. You want to teach your puppy as many good habits as possible before adolescence kicks in. The adolescent (juvenile) stage lasts from six months of age through two years of age. Your adolescent dog has an "I wanna be in charge" attitude just as much as a human teenager has. Early socialization teaches the dog you're the boss, which will help alleviate your frustration during this period.

Dogs reach adulthood by two years. If you've done your part to provide proper socialization and training, you'll end up with a well-behaved pet.

During all of these stages, beginning at birth, it's essential for puppies to be talked

to and handled by people. The breeder is the first person to teach puppies what people are like, so this role is crucial to proper socialization.

The Breeder's Role

Does it really matter where or from whom you get a dog? Absolutely! The benefits of purchasing a puppy from a reputable breeder extend beyond health certifications and the opportunity to evaluate the litter's parents for temperament and appearance. A good breeder makes a concerted effort to start socialization at birth. She handles the pups every day, orienting them to household goings-on, so they can transition to their new homes with confidence. Puppies raised with little human contact are shy

and less confident about new situations, making them dif-ficult to handle and train.

During their first month of life, puppies are most influ-enced by their mother and littermates, but human handling is still important. A puppy's first encounter with human touch is when the pup is born. The breeder picks the puppy up to clean it off, determine whether it's a boy or a girl, check that the puppy is whole and healthy, and place a piece of colored rickrack around the neck for identification.

Several times a day, a breeder handles the newborn pups to weigh them, ensure they're doing well, or give them a snuggle. The breeder also watches the puppies' mother (dam) to see how she reacts to people. If she welcomes human touch and lets people handle her babies, the pups will be accepting of human attention.

By the time a puppy is three weeks old, each day brings new lessons. The breeder should provide stimulation and encourage learning. Some ways to do so are to introduce the puppies to regular household sounds such as the whirr of a coffee grinder and the clatter of dishes. Sound effects tapes or CDs can give the puppies their first encounters with other noises, such as thunder and traffic.

Teaching through touch continues. A breeder should handle all parts of the dog's body—including the paws, teeth, tail, and genital area. Familiarizing puppies with this kind of handling prepares them for future veterinary and grooming visits and, for show dogs, inspection in the conformation ring.

If you know that your puppy will be exposed to certain sounds in your home, be sure the breeder introduces them before you bring your puppy home. It won't be too late to accustom her to certain noises once she's living with you, but the earlier she's aware of them, the better.

By five to seven weeks of age, puppies are curious explorers. This is a great time for the breeder to start introducing the pups to people beyond the family circle, including potential buyers and neighbors. It's at this age that puppies are most likely to make their first visit to the veterinarian for their initial vaccinations. Visiting the veterinarian is a great first opportunity for puppies to ride in the car, to meet and be handled by new people, and to experience new sounds and surfaces, such as the cold metal of an exam table. A good veterinarian will touch and talk to the puppy first to help relax her before beginning an exam

or giving any vaccinations. During the pup's second month, the breeder may also begin to introduce some basic training concepts. These can include spending time alone in a crate, pottying outdoors, wearing a real collar and leash, and respecting human family members by not chewing on them. Breeders who teach these concepts give their puppies a head start on success in their new homes.

Picking a Well-Socialized Puppy

When going to pick out your new puppy, it's easy to fall in love with the first pup who jumps up on your lap. But there's a lot more to consider, including your own personality and what type of personality you're looking for in a dog.

Start by looking at the dam. The father, or sire, may not live on site, but the dam and any other adult dogs the breeder has at her home give you a pretty clear picture of how the puppies will behave when they grow up.

Next, look at the puppies themselves. In any litter, there
are all types of personalities—there are calm pups who
make good companions if you're a couch potato and

energetic ones who make great competitors in dog sports or can be superb jogging partners. A good breeder should have a feel for each pup's personality and can help you choose the one who is right for you. In many cases, the breeder may interview you to help determine which puppy is best suited for you and your family.

Be wary of a puppy who shivers or seems distant or frightened when you pick him up. A puppy who freezes up at human touch or who is reluctant and fearful when placed on his back has clearly not been socialized. Do not select such a puppy. In fact, avoid purchasing any of the

puppies from the litter. If you notice similar behaviors by puppies in pet stores or shelters and suspect poor socialization as the cause, get your pet from a different source. Poor socialization often results in an unmanageable adult dog, so choose wisely from the start.

Even if your puppy stays with the breeder for the recommended first twelve weeks (or more), the socialization job isn't complete. You need to continue acquainting your puppy with new situations, people, and experiences throughout adolescence.

People to Meet, Places to Go

Introducing your puppy to a variety of people and places is the easiest way to start socializing her once you bring her home. Invite the neighbors over, one or two at a time so the puppy isn't overwhelmed. Ask guests to wear a hat or sunglasses; your puppy needs to learn that these items go on and come off.

It's especially important for your puppy to meet children of all ages. If you don't have children of your own, borrow some! Nieces, nephews, and kids of friends and neighbors will undoubtedly be glad to play with your puppy. Again, invite only a few at a time, and keep an eye on things to make sure the puppy doesn't become overstimulated. (Symptoms of an overwhelmed puppy include frantic running or pacing and piddling.) Young children should hold the puppy only when they're sitting on the floor so they won't accidentally drop the dog. If you have a willing friend who will let your puppy meet her baby, seize this opportunity. Even though the puppy becomes accustomed to the sounds of adult humans, the squeals and

cries of a baby and the size of a stroller can be alarming. Be sure to restrain the dog during the introduction, and have someone hold the baby for safety. (See the "Your Dog and a New Baby" chapter for additional information.)

A visit to the pet supply store is another good way for your pup to expand her knowledge of the world. Here, she'll likely encounter automatic doors, grocery carts, birds or reptiles in cages, fish in aquariums, all kinds of smells, and more people to pet her and talk to her. The clerks may even give her a treat. You can also carry treats with you so people can give them to your puppy. The idea is for her to look forward to meeting new friends. If she hasn't received all her vaccinations yet, carry her or place her in the cart so her paws don't touch the ground, which may harbor diseases and harmful organisms from other animals roaming the store.

Tote your pup along to outdoor shopping malls and on errands to pet-friendly businesses, such as the dry cleaners or the bank. If she isn't fully trained yet, carry her to prevent any potty accidents or misbehavior that might mar the visit.

Enroll in puppy kindergarten. These low-key classes are perfect for puppies between ten and twelve weeks of age. They learn the basics of good behavior in a fun atmosphere and meet lots of other puppies and people. A favorite game is pass the puppy, which involves passing each pup from one person to the next so each dog gets petted by a lot of different people. If you have a small dog, look for a class that offers free-play periods segregated by size. It's good for your puppy to meet dogs of all sizes, but a bigger dog can accidentally hurt a smaller one during play.

Meeting Other Animals

Take your pup out to meet other dogs in the neighborhood—as long as everyone's up-to-date on their vaccinations! Whenever possible, expose your puppy to dogs of different breeds and sizes as well as to both males and females. Until your puppy is older and more confident, though, try to keep him away from dogs who are aggressive toward other dogs. The goal right now is to build his confidence, not scare him to death. An early bad experience can leave a lasting impression.

If you have a cat, or simply want your puppy to be familiar with cats (always a good idea), make introductions slowly and cautiously. Cats tend to be suspicious of dogs, especially feisty little puppies, so give them a couple of days to assimilate your new pup's presence. For the first meeting, keep your puppy in a crate so the cat can see and smell him without fear. Once your cat has stopped hissing at the canine intruder, let the two meet nose to nose, with your puppy on leash so you can control any lunging at the cat. Make sure your cat always has an escape route, whether it's through an open door or up a cat tree. If the cat feels trapped, she might attack the puppy.

The Routine Life

Dogs like things to stay the same, so your puppy will settle in faster if she knows what to expect and when. Feed her, play with her, and take her out to potty regularly. She may not be able to tell time by the clock, but her sharp observational skills will help her adjust to a schedule.

When you're at home, tether her to you with a 4- to 6-foot leash. She'll learn your routine, and you'll see instantly if she's showing signs of wanting to go potty. This is a great way to bond with your puppy and learn her habits.

Because your puppy can't be at your side all the time, put her in her crate or exercise pen for quiet time so she gets used to spending short periods alone. She should also learn to stay comfortably with other people in other places. Ask dog-loving friends, family, or neighbors if they'd puppy-sit once in a while at their homes, or schedule brief stays at a doggy day care or a boarding kennel. This will prepare your dog for times when you travel and can't take her with you.

Prepare your dog for variations in her environment by teaching her to go up and down stairs and in and out of elevators. Encourage her to walk over unusual surfaces, such as metal grates, newspaper, and anything that wobbles when it's walked on. When a dog experiences these "challenges" early in her life, those challenges will become routine.

Accustom your puppy to bathing and grooming as well. Gently brush her or trim her nails when she's feeling relaxed, and try to make opportunities to show her that being in the water is fun. Summer is a great time to introduce her to water by providing a kiddie pool in your yard. If you don't have a yard or if you get your puppy during the colder months, a sink or bathtub with shallow warm water will do. Be sure to keep your puppy in a warm, draft-free area after bath or swimming time until she's completely

dry. A blow-dryer set on low will help speed up the drying process, but remember that it's a new noise and may startle your pup.

Car trips take some adjusting to as well. Take her for short rides when you're going to the drive-through window at the bank or a fast-food restaurant. To keep your puppy from disturbing you while driving or from flying through the windshield when you stop suddenly, confine her in a secured crate or keep her in place with a seat belt or car seat made for dogs. Look for one that has padded straps and latches into your seat belt system. If possible, the safest place for your dog to be seat belted is in the middle of the backseat. Dogs who get carsick in a crate may do better sitting up next to a window so they can see out.

If they're not properly socialized, dogs can become possessive over their toys and food. To prevent this, your puppy needs to learn that it's OK for you to take away these items. Teach her the *drop it* command by saying the phrase while removing a toy from her mouth. When she gives up her toy nicely, return it to her with a lot of praise. Say "easy" or "gentle" as she takes a treat from your hand, so she learns it's not OK to snap.

Your Dog and a New Baby

The only thing more exciting than bringing a new puppy home is bringing a new baby home. Whether your dog is a puppy or an adult, he'll be intensely curious about a new addition to the family. Here are some ways to help your dog welcome and adjust to the youngest family member.

Start getting your dog used to babies even before your baby is born. Find a sound effects CD that includes a recording of baby noises, or record the cries of a friend's newborn. If you have willing friends or family members with babies, let your dog see and sniff their children. Cuddle the baby while someone else holds the dog in order to prevent any unwanted slurps. Many

dogs seem to be fascinated by babies—or at least tolerant of them—so these meetings should go well.

Once your baby is born, get your dog used to his or her smell before bringing the baby home. Let the dog sniff at a blanket or clothing that bears the baby's scent. The dog will be curious about the new smell. Take this opportunity to pet him, give him a treat, and say, "good dog," while he sniffs away. When Mom comes home from the hospital, let her greet the dog first while someone else is holding the baby. Then, Mom should sit down and cuddle the infant while the dog sniffs. Don't hold the baby out to the dog; some dogs view this gesture as an offer of a toy, and they will act accordingly.

As much as possible, involve the dog in the baby's care. This can include letting him watch as you change the

baby's diaper or taking both of them for a walk, baby in stroller and dog on leash. And every dog loves baby cleanup duty—lying beneath the high chair and bolting down the food that falls to the floor. It won't be long before your dog has a new best friend. That said, your dog is not a baby-sitter. Never leave your dog and baby together without supervision, and be sure to give your dog extra attention whenever possible so that he doesn't feel neglected.

Introducing Adopted Dogs to a Multipet House

At some point, you may want to add a second dog to your family. Whether you acquire another puppy or adopt an adult dog from a shelter or breed rescue group, you'll want to make proper introductions to help the new relationship get off on the right paw. It's also important to be patient and positive and provide the new dog with a routine.

Let the dogs meet in neutral territory, such as a park or a friend's home. With both dogs on a loose leash, each with her own handler, let them sniff each other while talking to them in a happy tone. A loose leash promotes confidence and ease. Tension on the leash suggests something to be worried about. Walk the dogs around and let them each perform a couple of simple commands so you can reward them. Meeting new canine friends should be fun!

Once they've had a little while to get to know each other and seem to be getting along (exhibiting play bows rather than prolonged stares), you can make the trek home. Walk them home if you're close enough; otherwise, load them up in the car. Ideally, both dogs will ride in sep-

arate crates, but if that's not possible, secure them in their own spots: for instance, put one on each side of the backseat, or put one in the backseat and one in the front. When you arrive, let them spend some time together in the yard, supervised, before you enter the house.

To prevent jealousy, each dog should have her own crate, dishes, and toys. Feed the dogs in their crates or in separate areas to avoid food aggression. Give plenty of love and attention to your first dog so she knows she hasn't been replaced. Have separate play and training sessions with each dog, but provide time for group interac-

tion, too. This satisfies their needs for individual attention and your need for them to work and play well together.

If you're introducing a puppy to an older dog, make allowances for each dog's potential issues. An older dog may not enjoy having a puppy constantly climbing over her. Give the older dog a place she can retreat to when she's had too much, or crate the puppy so the older dog can have some time on her own or with you. A puppy is still learning her place in the family pack. Don't leave her alone with older dogs until she's fully integrated into the home. For some dogs, this takes as little as a day or two, but for others, the get-acquainted period can last for weeks or months. Until your new dog seems to be accepted or is of an appropriate size to take care of herself, crate one or both dogs when you leave them alone.

Dogs are social critters at heart, and most of them enjoy company. In most cases, your dog will welcome the companion- ship of another  dog or even a cat. That will most likely be the case if you've taken the time to socialize her to new people, animals, objects, and experiences.

Conclusion

A puppy's early experiences affect his entire life. Socialize your puppy from the day you bring him home; when he is old, you both will continue to benefit from it. Make a list of all the things you want your puppy to know about, such as cats, blenders, treadmills, golf carts, country music, people in uniform, men wearing baseball caps, teens on skateboards, other dogs, children in strollers, people using crutches or wheelchairs, automatic doors, and people petting or grooming him on all parts of his body. The list is endless. Then make sure you introduce these elements during your puppy's first weeks with you.

The best socialization advice? Go at your puppy's pace, keep things positive, and make sure he's having fun. You can't beat the result: a new best friend who can go almost anywhere with you, who loves meeting new people and animals, and who loves and respects you.

Kim Campbell Thornton is an award-winning writer and editor. During her tenure as editor of *Dog Fancy*, the magazine won three Dog Writers Association of America Maxwell Awards for best all-breed magazine. Her book *Why Do Cats Do That?* was named best behavior book in 1997 by the Cat Writers Association. Kim is the author of the Simple Solutions series books *Aggression*, *Barking*, *Chewing*, *Digging*, and *House-Training*. She is also the former president of the Cat Writers Association.

Buck Jones's humorous illustrations have appeared in numerous magazines (including *Dog Fancy* and *Cat Fancy*) and books. He is the illustrator for the best-selling Simple Solutions series books; *Why Do Cockatiels Do That?*; *Why Do Parakeets Do That?*; *Kittens! Why Do They Do What They Do?*; and *Puppies! Why Do They Do What They Do?* Contact Buck through his Web site: http://www.buckjonesillustrator.com.